THE WRITINGS OF

WILL ROGERS

I - 5

SPONSORED BY

The Will Rogers Memorial Commission
and Oklahoma State University

THE WRITINGS OF WILL ROGERS

OTHER VOLUMES TO BE ANNOUNCED

ROGERS-ISMS

The Cowboy Philosopher

on

PROHIBITION

By Will Rogers

Joseph A. Stout, Jr., *Editor*

Peter C. Rollins, *Assistant Editor*

OKLAHOMA STATE UNIVERSITY PRESS
Stillwater, Oklahoma
1975

Note to scholars: The Harper & Brothers book and the original illustrations are reproduced with permission of the Will Rogers Memorial Commission, Claremore, Oklahoma, and The Rogers Company, Beverly Hills, California. The scholarly apparatus and notes in this volume are copyrighted and the usual rules about the use of copyrighted material apply.

(Illustrations courtesy Will Rogers Memorial, Claremore, Oklahoma)

International Standard Book Number 0-914956-06-X

Library of Congress Catalog Number 75-21295

Printed in the United States of America

CONTENTS

INTRODUCTION

Prohibition: The "Noble Experiment"

The Cowboy Philosopher on Prohibition cannot be appreciated properly without some contextual information about the social experiment it satirized. Prohibitionists had won many regional battles for more than a century prior to the passage of the 18th Amendment. By 1914, fifteen states had voted complete prohibition into law, and almost one-half of the population and three fourths of the area of the United States already had prohibited liquor by the drink.

World War One offered the advocates of prohibition a special opportunity, for the nation was put on a system of voluntary rationing. Prohibitionists used the rationing campaign to portray distillers and brewers as unpatriotic. Every bottle of bourbon, every bottle of beer—so the argument ran—represented potential foodstuffs for our Allies in Europe. As Maude Radford Warren, a prohibitionist advocate, explained, "Every man who works on the land to produce drink instead of bread is a loss in winning the War; and worse, he may mean a dead soldier." Other super patriots equated the German habit of drinking beer with sympathy for the enemy. Liquor was proclaimed "the Kaiser's mightiest ally." When all other arguments failed, prohibitionists observed that the efficiency of American workers was seriously impaired by what was called "blue Monday absenteeism."

The prohibition movement played upon the anxieties of native Americans during this period. Urban political machines were accused of purchasing the immigrant vote with whiskey. Native Americans who believed they saw erosion of their political dominance joined with prohibitionists to close saloons in order to remove this lubricant for political corruption. In the South prohibition was seen as a form of social control which anxious whites aimed specifically at their black neighbors. Prohibitionists easily convinced urban manufacturers with immigrant work forces that workers would work more effectively if demon rum could be kept out of their hands during leisure time. The passage of the 18th Amendment culminated the campaign against disorder, lawlessness, and sloth.

Americans quickly learned that forcing a law through a legislature did not guarantee obedience from an independent people. Four thousand federal officers were employed to enforce the Volstead Act. Yet despite countless raids and prosecutions, the transportation and consumption of the forbidden beverages continued. (Ironically, nearly ten per cent of the law enforcement officers were dismissed for accepting bribes from bootleggers!) Especially vexing was the problem of dealing with a home-brewing spree which swept the country. Stills were sold openly in shops, and as Will Rogers described at length in his book, the cellar suddenly became a place of interest for the man of the house.

Undoubtedly, prohibition was responsible for nuturing organized crime. With general approbation, mobsters performed the public service of supplying liquor, a feat legitimate businesses were unable to accomplish. By the mid-twenties, informed individuals estimated that an immigrant named Al Capone had gained complete control of Cicero, a Chicago suburb. Within this fiefdom, saloons flourished with little fear of legal interference. The Capone gang performed "public services" on a very large scale, and they probably realized beer and whiskey sales amounting to more than fifty million dollars. The Capone group alone may have collected more than twenty-million dollars for other illicit "services." Gradually, the American public realized that prohibition was a futile attempt to legislate morality, and that it was economically too expensive to continue. The economic argument for legalizing the sale of alcoholic beverages became especially convincing as the depression of the thirties deepened. Ultimately, the Democrats in control of Congress repealed prohibition after Franklin D. Roosevelt assumed office in 1933.

Will Rogers' attitude toward the futility of prohibition was undoubtedly influenced by his early experience with the "noble experiment." Rogers was born in Indian Territory where it was intermittently illegal to manufacture or sell liquor — especially to Indians. When Indian Territory became the state of Oklahoma in 1907 the Constitution established legal prohibition. Throughout the Prohibition era, Rogers was critical of any government trying to regulate morals. The cowboy philosopher lived long enough to see Oklahoma allow the sale of 3.2% beer in 1933, but it was 1959 before the state passed an amendment to repeal prohibition in Oklahoma.

Will Rogers on Prohibition

Will Rogers signed his first book contract during the last week of May, 1919. Harper and Brothers Publishing Company wanted to issue in inexpensive editions (60 cents each) six short volumes of Rogers' gags. However, the only two volumes completed were *The Cowboy Philosopher on the Peace Conference* and *The Cowboy Philosopher on Prohibition* (which came out a month later). Numerous personal letters and articles written prior to 1919 (available at the Will Rogers Memorial, Claremore, Oklahoma) show that Rogers was capable of a more literate style than what appeared in these two volumes. While the introductions were authentic, most of the material in these books were isolated "gags" taken from his stage act, or adapted from working notes. Moreover, Rogers' comments on stage were mostly ad-lib and he played to the audience—switching, changing ,and adding material according to what "went over". The effectiveness of a line often depended as much on the manner of delivery as its contents. Thus these volumes contain Rogers' material, but shaped into book style by editors at Harper and Brothers rather than by Rogers.

Although the final form of the work might not have been exactly what Rogers prepared, the Oklahoman's ability to say things in a witty and clear fashion still was evident. For example, he utilized parallels between the names of the major participants in World War One and their national liquors. In this manner he suggested a fanciful casual relationship between the intake of alcohol and the Allied wartime victories:

> France fought quite a bit in the war and trained on Wine, England did her part on Scotch and Polly and Ale, Canadian Club furnished its Quota from Canada, Italy Chiantied over the Alps into Austria, Womens clothes and Scotch Whiskey dident keep the Highlanders back much Guinnesses Stout kept the Irish fighting as usual, the American troops dident retreat any further than you can run your hand in a Paper Bag, And they had been used to old Crow and Kentucky Bourbon, Russia was doing fine till some nut took their Vodka away from them and they went back to look for it and nobody has ever heard of them since, Germany the Country with the smallest percentage of Alcohol in their National drink (which is beer) and Turkey who are totally prohibition—why they lose the war.

In fact, few people realized how well Rogers' writing would be accepted later. The cowboy philosopher even "poked fun" at himself, for in his introduction to this volume he remarked, "you

wont find the Country any drier than this book."
But Rogers' humor was far more perceptive than
he wanted to admit. For example, in one of the
"frothier" passages of this work on Prohibition,
Rogers trifled at length with the idea of lightness,
specifically in terms of the inferior beer brewed
during the war and after it: "if they can get beer
any lighter than it is they will have to get a prop
to hold it up. Have to turn your glass upside down
not to keep it from flying away." But just as pun-
gently, Rogers unraveled an idea such as the con-
cept of political purification through the absurd to
an insight which required his audience to think:
"They used to say, drive the saloons out of politics,
why not go further and drive politics out of Congress." In this last statement, there was a momen-
tary glimpse of the serious side of Rogers, the
Rogers who, for all his laughs at the "game" of
politics, was contemptuous of anything short of the
highest performance. This was the philosophically
sober Rogers who smuggled in a judgment when
he said: "Bout the only thing left for a poor man
that cant afford his own house with a cellar is to
move to a Republic."

Rogers often chose to teach his lessons by indirec-
tion and parable rather than by precept. In *The
Cowboy Philosopher on Prohibition,* drawing from
an item in the daily news, Rogers reported: "Convict in Toronto Canada waiting to be hung gave
his guard some coffee, and a powder in it that put
him to sleep and the fellow escaped, prohibitionists
now use that against coffee drinking habit." The
moral of this story was obvious, but Rogers left it
unstated: anything in public domain can be mis-
used, but this does not constitute a *prima facie*
argument for government restriction. Later in the
same book, Rogers explored the absurdity of the
Eighteenth Amendment, when he discussed it in
terms of how it would affect American women   xvii

(who had recently gained the right to vote through the Nineteenth Amendment). Viewed with an innocent eye, the success both of the Eighteenth and Nineteenth amendments seemed to constitute a peculiar trade of rights: "Now Congress says the women can vote. They use to could drink and not vote now they can vote and not drink." As with so many contemporary events, Rogers looked for the particular human discomforts and problems which resulted: "It will take them just as long to make up their minds who to vote for as it did to tell what to order to drink. Most of them will vote for some guy named Martini just through force of habit." Will Rogers in this remark was perhaps guilty of what has been in the seventies called "male chauvinism"; his focus on particular human beings rather than abstractions raises a significant point about the two amendments. While Americans solemnly were congratulating themselves for giving women the right to vote, they were at the same time guilty of passing an essentially anti-libertarian amendment through humorous human detail rather than an abstract statement. As a result, he made his point more persuasively.

With an acute awareness of the ridiculous, Rogers explored the numerous changes Prohibition introduced into American life. Families would find new subjects for quarrels ("the worst crime a child at home can commit now is to eat up the raisins that Dad brought home for fermenting purposes"). But Rogers humorously conceded that Prohibition had its positive side: roads were flourishing where no amount of pleading could have encouraged building in the past; and husbands all over the country were becoming more attentive to their household tasks, especially tasks which took them down to the basement.

Yet for all his humorous play with the petty irritations of Prohibition, Rogers was seriously unhappy about the ignobility of the "noble experiment." As a spokesman for an older and more secure America, Rogers remembered a different sort of political leadership than that which had helped pass the Volstead Act: "There is an old legend that years ago there was a man elected to Washington who voted according to his own conscience." Thus what value *The Cowboy Philosopher on Prohibition* has above its ability to entertain lies in Rogers' exposure of the hypocrisy which became a necessary outgrowth of legislation aimed at influencing personal morality. His extended development of the story of Noah's Ark successfully ridiculed the religious arguments in favor of prohibition. His accurate reading of the enforcement records of Kansas and Maine invalidated the anti-crime arguments. His quick twist of the argument in favor of prohibition as a guard to the American home was devastating: "It wont stop divorces it will stop marriages . . . A couple sitting opposite a table dont look near so good to each other over a water decanter as they do over two just emptied Champaign glasses." While Rogers indicated that he might have endorsed President Wilson's program (no liquor by the drink, but sales in stores for home consumption) , his major complaint against Prohibition was that it worked to reward hypocrisy rather than honesty. Instead of voting on principle, "wet" politicians supported the reform because they felt that it might win a few votes back home. Prohibition was self-defeating because it made liquor appear more attractive than it would be without legal restrictions. Finally, the resulting intrusion of government into the pattern of personal life threatened to turn America up-side-down: "The only way you could tell a Citizen from a Bootlegger in Kansas was the Bootlegger would be sober."

If Rogers' books of 1919 are considered as companion volumes, then the ultimate irony of the immediate post-war era is underscored dramatically. In *The Cowboy Philosopher on the Peace Conference,* Will Rogers traced the political ineptitude, dishonesty, and rapacity which made the treaty of Versailles such a hated document and President Wilson's idealistic League of Nations such a failure with the American people. Ironically, the same period saw the passage of the Volstead Act, an essentially worthless and negative swipe by rural America at Sin and the Cities. For this reason, Rogers was not entirely after a laugh when he said at the conclusion of *The Cowboy Philosopher on Prohibition* that "If Pres Wilson wanted to get this League of Nations through he should have taken some Prohibitionists with him and they would have showed him how to get it through whether the people wanted it or not." Over the next sixteen years in his role as a journalist, Will Rogers attempted to expose subsequent confusion of priorities and misuse of the legislative process. Later, more substantial volumes of the *Writings of Will Rogers* will show clearly how attentive and vocal Rogers was about hypocrisy and rhetoric in American life.

THE EDITORS

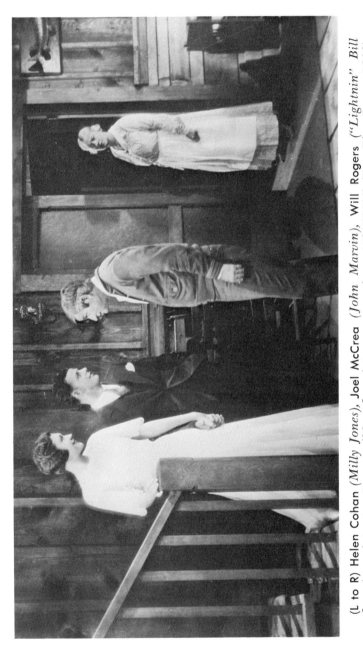

(L to R) Helen Cohan (*Milly Jones*), Joel McCrea (*John Marvin*), Will Rogers (*"Lightnin'" Bill Jones*), and Louise Dresser (*Mrs. Jones*) in a scene from LIGHTNIN' (Fox Film Corp., 1930).

PREFACE

My first meeting with Will Rogers was in 1930 at Lake Tahoe, where Will was on location making *Lightnin'* of which he was the star. Will was one of Fox Studio's biggest stars and the director, Henry King, asked me if I would like to meet him. Will was sitting in a buggy flicking the flies off a horse. The director said, "Will, I want you to meet Joel McCrea. He is going to play your son-in-law." Will looked over kind of quick and said, "Get in Joel and sit down." I climbed in the buggy and sat down and from that moment on there was a kind of feeling of comradeship that lasted as long as Will was here with us. That comradeship and the immediate interest Will showed in me and my future secured me from that time on in the motion picture business, and also greatly influenced my life. I learned so much from him it would take a whole book to tell it all, but one of the most important things I learned was behavior in life.

Of course, being able to work with Will was uplifting. The people at Fox had a regard and respect for him as a great American. Everybody, from the other stars to the camera crew, gaffers, electricians, and extras wanted Will to have a regard for him. He was important to everybody. There was an atmosphere around every place he worked and it seemed as if everything he touched had a little more glory after he touched it. I guess that is the key word—glory. He glorified everything. For example, when he came into a studio with a lot of actors and actresses already there, Life came with him. He made things seem vital and important. The behavior on the set, the attitude toward foreigners, the behavior toward minority groups, all this would subtly change. Without ever saying or demanding anything, Will, by his example, made these things right. He glorified them. His tremendous enthusiasm, courage, and dignity, not to mention humor, in everything he said and did was one of the greatest examples I ever saw. I remember him telling me, "Joel, you got only one life to live . . . life should be lived, not just existed",

I think that anybody who really stands for something and has great strength of character has an effect on people. Will Rogers did nothing to make himself popular. He just told you what he thought from his heart and that made him popular because you knew he was sincere and you knew he stood for the right thing. He was motivated by this "right consciousness" and his love for people. He became the voice of the people by expressing himself sincerely—and his humorous expression of himself was something that caught on and pleased everybody. Will's humor was timely and interesting, his common-sense philosophy has held up through the years. He saw that he had a function, and he used humor more and more to show people their hypocrisies. Will Rogers was an individual—an original. He didn't copy anyone nor conform to anything. He had the tremendous talent and ability to make people see their own faults and yet not injure their dignity.

The last deep impression I had of Will was that he was getting a little tired of acting, as such. What he really wanted to do was fly. He wanted to see what the Russians were doing. He wanted to see the world and see what the world was doing. He read every available paper, and he was interested in everything. He wanted to rope, to play polo, to fly, to act, to talk about politics, and to write his column. He was a man of tremendous energy and activity. When we were working on the movie set and it got to be time to go home, instead of saying good night and leaving like most of the stars did, he would say, "Santa Monica Canyon, let's really knock on it." And every time I saw him on the lot or at a rodeo he used to give a little yell—a lot of cowboys will remember it—it was something like this—"*Yahaaa . . . .*" Will used to yell like that when he was pleased to see somebody and I will never forget it—and I guess I will always keep listening for it.

When Will said his famous "I never met a man I didn't like," it could also be said that he never met a man that didn't like him. How America misses him today with the problems we have. My feeling is that the more we can read about him and think about him and keep him alive in our hearts the better off we will all be. I always felt **Will** belonged to the world and I am not trying to **impress** anyone with how well I knew him because **basically** what he lived to say and what he lived to **do is** as available to you as it is to me. I am very fortunate and very grateful that I was able to be with him, but the great value he has is still alive in his books.

I hope you will enjoy reading this publication of Will's little book on Prohibition. This isn't much of an introduction but things I have recalled are so vivid in my memory I had to say it.

Joel McCrea

The Cowboy Philosopher
on *PROHIBITION*

I-5

THE 14 POINTS OF THE PREAMBLE

ALL high class Literary Lizzards when they start assembling a book have some fellow that is better known than they are to dash off a kind of an introduction, Well I was afraid if I had someone do that they would just be liable to say something funny And out side of the book being SHORT the one thing I guarantee it to be free from is humor, I dont want anybody spoiling the Book with some Komical remarks,

Besides I carry my own introductions with me, For I figure that no man can give you as good a boost as you can give yourself,

I would not have written this Book but My Publishers (get that, my Publishers) Harper and Brothers, (by mentioning their name they wont cut this out) Big firms love advertising just as much as us little punks do,[1]

My Publishers asked me to write another Book as they had a sale on the last one, (Which was called Will Rogers on the Peace

1

*Conference) Dont hurt to slip in a little Add
for yourself once in awhile Especially when
it is done in a clever way like this and dont
look like one,*

They said write another book as we have
traced the sale of the last one, And the fellow
who bought it has a friend in the same in-
stitution, And we feel sure we can double
the sale of your last book with this one,

In tracing this sale they found the party
who bought the book was the same one who
voted annually for Bryan,[2] And his friend
who we hope to land as a prospective pur-
chaser, Holds the proud distinction of being
the only man in the United States who found
no fault with Burleson,[3]

I said to them what will I write about,
And they said by all means pick out a subject
that is different, Something that nobody else
has written on, Get something where you
have no opposition, Well I started to think-
ing, then one night it came to me, I give you

2

my word I had not heard a word about it, neither had I read anything in any papers about it, I dont know myself how I happened to think of it, But I got right up and wired my Publishers

"Have-hit-on-just-the-thing,-an-original-sub-ject,-PROHIBITION"

Aint it wonderful how I just happened to hit on this out of the way subject, and Title, Of course a writer must not let his Title interfere with what he is writing about, Look at that Spaniard he wrote a Book called the "Four Horse men of the Apothecary" I read it plum through and there wasent a thing about Horses or Drug Stores or anybody riding, In fact there is no town or Country on the map where these four fellows are supposed to come from, Then he has another book called Blood and Sand[4] and its all about Horses and Cattle,

Now the Title of this little Gem of Free Thought is PROHIBITION But I will be like the Spaniard, The more I can keep my readers away from the Title, And keep them just on the opposite from the Title (about 95 proof) why the more chance I got getting away with it,

I want also to regretfully announce that this Book is not subsidized by any Liquor Concern,

You wont find the Country any drier than this Book,

All Stage rights of material in this Book reserved for Senators and Congressmen to tell at Chautauquas[5] as original,

Want to thank Proffessor Lowell[6] of Harvard for the English Translation

Want also to thank the Writers of the Old and new Testament for furnishing facts for

4

some of my strongest Arguments against Prohibition,

PROHIBITION

NOW before I start in I want it distinctly understood I dont knock Prohibition through any personal grudge as I do not drink myself, But I do love to play to an audience who have had a few nips, just enough so they can see the joke and still sober enough to applaud it,[7]

You all who have had no experience have no Idea of the difference, the Prohibitionists just seem to be sore on the World,

How they got the thing through, Senators and Congressmen were all in Washington waiting for the next pay day, When one member come in and says lets vote on Prohibition, The others all said, Why we cant vote on Prohibition our people back home dident tell us to come here and vote Prohibition, The old desciple of Bryan democracy that had proposed it says No I know they dident tell us to vote on it but its a good day and I just feel like voting on something,[8]

So they sent around to all the various Bars in Washington and collected a quorum and voted everybody dry,

They did not know when they were doing it that they were killing off the thing that a Senator or Congressman holds dearer than anything in the World And that is an Audience in the Galleries in Washington, For no one ever goes to hear them any more, In fact no man living can sit in the Gallery and listen to them without a certain amount of Liquor in him,

They dident want to vote dry but they were so afraid of the way the Political Breeze seemed to be headed at the time, Never figuring it might change,

There is an old Legend that years ago there was a man elected to Washington *who* voted according to his own conscience,

Congressmens short sightedness is what put it through, then Bryan modestly claimed the credit,

They claim it was necessary to put it through as a war measure, how about this? Now France fought quite a bit in the war and trained on Wine, England did her part on Scotch and Polly and Ale, Canadian Club

8

furnished its Quota from Canada, Italy Chiantied over the Alps into Austria, Womens clothes and Scotch Whiskey dident keep the Highlanders back much Guinnesses Stout kept the Irish fighting as usual, The American Troops dident retreat any further than you can run your hand in a **Paper Bag,** And they had been used to old Crow and Kentucky Bourbon, Russia was doing fine till some nut took their Vodka away from them and thay went back to look for it and nobody has ever heard of them since, Germany the Country with the smallest percentage of Alcahol in their National drink (which is beer) and Turkey who are totally prohibition, —why they lose the war,

Looks to me like if Germany and Turkey ever wanted to win a war they better start drinking a MANS SIZE DRINK,

Now a Prohibitionist is a man or woman, Who is so self satisfied with himself that he presents himself with a Medal, called the "CROIX DE PERFECT HE"

He gives himself this Medal because he is now going to start to meddle in everybodys business but his own,

9

Look at these Towns and people after Prohibition has hit them, Everybody looks like they had just had a puncture and no extra tire,

Streets that used to be lighted up at nights and thousands of people on them are now used for robbing purposes only,

If you drop into a Cafe after the Theater in a Prohibition town, They will wake up the Night watchman to cook you something,

Watch a crowd clustered around a couple of water pitchers in the center of the Table, They look like they had just heard the Kaiser had invaded Belgium again,

It will take some men two years solid rehersing to learn how to order a soft drink without blushing,

I knew one man in a dry town when he took his first Grape Juice high ball; it took three Doctors to revive him,

Somebody ought to get out a book **"How to learn to drink soft drinks in 20 lessons,"**

10

Soda Fountains will all have to go to the extra expense now of putting in a foot rail,

There will be people among the coming generation that can name 12 different Phosphates that couldent name 2 Presidents,

The first six ice cream sodas served to six pinockle players mean six more Bolshevikis,

One good thing in favor of the soda squirt bartender, His trade dont start coming in as early in the morning as the old hard stuff ones did,

The new ice cream dipper hound at the fountain will have another advantage over the old bartender, he wont have to listen to the same story over and over again,

If prohibition will just stop some men trying to repeat stories they have heard, It will not have been in vain,

Once they claim a fellow repeated a story he had heard and got it right, but this has never been verified,

11

If they will bring the ice cream into the drug stores in kegs instead of tins, They will make a lot of men seem more at home,

They will soon be listing Jamaica Ginger[9] stock on the exchange,

They are trading Bethleham steel shares now for Peruna stock and paying the difference,

When a man drives up to a Gasoline filling station he will say, Give me 10 gallons in the tank and fill up this pint bottle,

The worst crime a child at home can commit now is to eat up the raisins that Dad brought home for fermenting purposes,

If I was California I would not claim the credit for making the wine they are serving nowadays,

Just look at the industries that will be put out of business, Getting bit by a snake will be a lost art,

You know no man is going to let a snake bite him after Liquor goes out,

12

Then there is the woman who used to faint and Brandy seemed to be the only thing that would revive her, now she will have to struggle along without fainting,

But the saddest case of all will be the loss of the Kentucky Colonel industry (They received their title through owning the widest brimmed black hat and having the largest Bourbon capacity of any man in the county Sah,)

When they go to dig up his Mint bed, He will say just dig it a little deeper and I will get in myself, we are both nonessentials,

Of course on the other hand it has introduced a lot of new methods especially in regard to getting it in to dry territory, There are people who if they put in half the time studying on some mechanical invention that they do how to smuggle in booze, Why they would be as great as Edison,[10]

They put it in extra tires and even in the ones they were running on, One day a fellow had a couple of blow outs on the way into Oklahoma and lost all the profits,

13

But there is really only one successful way to bring it into dry territory and after all it is the most satisfactory, You drink it just before you get to the state line, in this way you are allowed to bring in all you can carry,

I saw a box of Armours Meat drop off an express wagon and broke every bottle,

Prohibition has done some very good things in the road building line, It has been the cause of more road improvement between dry and wet towns than any other thing,

If you want good roads leading out of your town vote it wet and the surrounding towns will fix up your roads,

Bad roads have broke more bottles of booze than the authorities,

The Prohibitionists put the bill through as a food saving device, And it has certainly been a success, Its made food so high people cant eat it,

The poorer people will have to go to Europe this summer to escape the high prices over here,

It looks like we would have to have another war for things to get cheap like they used to be during the last one,

And they still allow these Prohibitionists to eat, You know a drinking man he dont eat much and the more he drinks the less he eats but these Prohibitionists they just naturally ruin a meal,

Prohibitionists dispose of enough food just before speaking engagements to feed all the starving Armenians in the world,[11]

The amount of time and energy consumed by Prohibitionists in speaking if put to a legitimate business would cut everybodys average work day down to 4 hours,

But the minute they get Prohibition they will hop on to something else it will be Cigarettes or room and bath, or something

See where they propose to stop Cigarettes first and then profanity, They are going to have a tough time with that profanity, cause as long as there is a prohibitionist living there will be profanity, !ZR-Z*??ZIZ,!R-R-R-Z!!!

You have seen millions and millions of dollars worth of Liberty Bonds sold in Cafes where everybody is drinking and jolly, Did you ever see any sold in an Ice Cream Parlor,

The government said a man in Uniform couldent get a drink, Guess the government figured that the ones who dident have the nerve to go needed the liquor worse than the soldiers did,

Headlines in papers last year said **"Government stopped Brewries making beer"** The brewries had stopped making BEER years ago of their own accord,

On account of the bartenders diluting the drinks people were ready for prohibition before they knew it,

If they stall off Prohibition from July to january some bars will have to get another bottle of booze,

16

Mighty good thing we have had a nice warm winter this year or people would not have had any room in their Cellars for their coal,

Next winter there will be husbands tending to furnaces that never knew where they were before,

What is life without a cellar

If a residence gets on fire nowadays the fireman dont run to save the children or the valuables but to the cellar to save the booze,

There has been more underground building in the last year than there has been on top,

Prohibition has been a big saving for a lot of fellows. Where they used to have to go to the corner, now they only have to go down stairs,

If you ever see this add in the papers they would have to call out all the police reserves to keep back the applicants, "FOR SALE ONE HOUSE FULLY STOCKED,"

17

Bout the only thing left for a poor man that cant afford his own house with a cellar is to move to a Republic,

Personally I think the saloon men put this prohibition through as they have sold more in the last year than in any ten previous years before,

Every time the Government would put on an extra tax the liquor people would put two extra on for themselves,

Industries that switched to making ammunition during the war are now trying to see if they cant manufacture some drink called NO KICKO, or PRETTY NEAR O,

Everybody wonders what to do with the Kaiser, I think he should be brought over here and made to sample every soft drink made,

Maine and Kansas were the first Prohibition states, now look at them,[12]

Maine was noted for two things, one was drinking awful whiskey and the other was shooting another hunter,

18

If it had not been for the hunting season in Maine and the early deaths from bad whiskey, Maine would have had a population now almost equal to Rhode Island,

The principal industry of Kansas was bootlegging,

The only way you could tell a **Citizen** from a **Bootlegger** in Kansas was the **Bootlegger** would be sober,

"There was so many bl nd P gs n Kansas for years that the Nat ve hog of that State today s born w thout eyes,"

The Booze they sold was so strong they had to dilute it with Alcahol,

Light Wines and Beers were as little known there, as Bevo[13] is in a wet state,

Champaigne was as rare as a bathtub,

The liquor was made from corn without either shucking or shelling it,

19

This high explosive they used in the war called T N T, was originally Bootleg Whisky,

If a Bootlegger finds his supply running low he adds a hand full of Giant Powder and a few bottles of red ink and serves,

If a state ever once goes dry it will stay, as there is enough Whisky peddlers to keep it voted that way,

Imagine voting the Nation dry when the Allies owe all their success now to Haig and the Tanks,[14]

They say the Tanks over there would go through anything, Well we have Tanks over here that have gone through all they ever had,

Convict in Toronto Canada waiting to be hung gave his guard some coffee, had a powder in it that put him to sleep and the fellow escaped, prohibitionists now use that against coffee drinking habit,

I just want to sight a case what a wrong prohibition coming into a country will do and the pleasures and amusements it will knock people out of seeing, I got a friend Bill Rice runs a Carnival Company had the first one of these diving girl shows, Well he went to a little town in Arizona to play and got all ready, dug the hole and put his tank in and was all ready for the water when they told him why there wasent that much water in the whole county, and was just about to crab the show when an old saloon man said he could fill it up with CORN WHISKY, it would look like water, so they did and that afternoon when the act went on Bill himself was the first out on the diving board, nobody up to then knew Bill could dive but he sho did, and went off that board mighty pretty but dident come up so they all waited and finally ran to the edge and looked over and there lay Bill high and dry on the bottom just sucking up the last that was in the tank, Now those people away out there if prohibition had been in would have been denied that exhibition, and diving was an awful big novelty to them, and it also taught Bill a lesson, If he ever went back to Arizona again to get a bigger tank,

Did you know that a prohibitionist could be arrested for treason, Treason means anything that gives annoyance to your own people thereby giving aid to the enemy,

21

Outside of profiteers I cant think of anything that has given more annoyance,

Prohibitionists are the originators of Camouflage, They made drinking look worse than it is,

The minute prohibition goes in, I can see Cincinnati ceceeding from the Union[15]

Ohio was voted wet by the people and dry by their missrepresentatives,

She was supposed to go dry a month ahead of the National ammendment She did that so it would give them a month to reherse in,

Pretty tough on the Columbus Ohio saloon men they have to close just when that big Methodist Conference meets there,[16]

The minute Prohibition went in my friend Luke Mcgluke claimed exemption,

Billy Sunday[17] (by the way I wonder what ever become of him) said when we get prohibition that there wont be any more jails,

Kansas and Maine have more in them than out,

Another thing it wouldent be right by those jailers to throw them out of a job, those prohibitionists never have any regard for the other people Just think of it the minute we get prohibition hundreds and hundreds of jailers and guards are thrown out of work,

Of course the only way we have to prove anything is by the Bible, I find Genesis 9th Chapter 20 verse, "Noah began to be an Husbandman and planted a vineyard,"

The minute he got to be a husband he started in right away to raise the necessary ingredients to make what goez with married life,

Now Californians followed Noahs example, But fortunately in Noahs time there was no one to tell him he couldent have a vineyard,

Why dont they pick on the Marrying thats in the same verse, why single out the poor old vineyard

23

Next Verse "And he drank of the wine and was drunken and was within his tent"

Now here is what shows the prohibitionist up so bad, for Noah was a chosen man, If the lord dident punish him where do they come in to tell somebody what to do,

The prohibitionists *rave* about water, Now Noah knew more about water than all of them put togeather, He was the WATER COMMISSIONER of his time, He was an expert on water and the first man smart enough *not* to drink it,

He was the first one to discover a use for it, that was to float a boat on, But as a beverage he knew it was a total failure,

Now everything happens for the best through Noah partaking of too much wine, and going on this little spree is why the lord picked him to gather these Animals into the Ark, He was the only one who had ever seen them,

You see if Noah had not drank we would today perhaps be without menageries,

24

Other men of later generations have claimed that they have seen animals that Noah dident take on the ark, But perhaps their Vineyards too were of a different variety,

Noah was told to collect two of every variety of animal and take them on board I defy any man to show me where he took a prohibitionist and his mate aboard,

The only thing we can liken in this day to the ark was the first commuting trip of George Washington, There was two of every kind of peace deligate with the exception of the Republican, there was only one of that specie, as there seemed to be at that time no especial desire on the part of the organizers of the expedition to populate the earth in the future with that kind of animal, As they propagate very fast,[18]

It is not even recorded in the history of the conference that they even landed there with this lone specimen, As theres been no mention made of him whatever,

In the next verse we find "Ham saw his father and told his bretheren"

25

There was the foundation of the first prohibitionist, butting in where he had no business,

He made such a bad job out of it thats why all bad actors are called hams,

In the next verse Noah awakes, puts a curse on Hams son Cannan, "and told him a servant of servants **shall ye be**"

Little did Noah think when he told him he would be a servant that some day servants would rule the house as they do today,

This wine had such ill effects on Noahs health that it was all he could do to live 950 years,

Just 19 years short of Methusalah who held the long distance age record of his and all time,

Show me a total abstainer that ever lived that long,

And on the 40th day Noah sent out a dove and unlike Bryans, Noahs came back,[19]

Now later on in the 14 chapter when Abram was returning from victorious battle it says Melchizedek king of salem met them with bread and wine,

What did we meet our victorious troops with Huylers Chocolate and spearmint chewing gum,

Also, shows that no matter what a long name a king may have there is some good in him,

What did Moses say when he took all the philistines up on top of the mountain He said "Corinthians what will you have"

And Rebecca with the pitcher who was it told her "fillem up again"

You only hear wine spoken of in there and that is as it should be now, Light wines and Beers, that was what they had in Biblical days and that is what President Wilson[20] says we should have, do away with the Hard Stuff, Also, can the saloons,

27

They used to say, drive the saloons out of politics, Why not go further and drive politics out of Congress,

I agree with the prohibitionists about doing away with Saloons and Whisky, But let people who want to, buy beer and light wines and take it to their homes and have it when they like,

If they would make all these fat saloon owners go to work, that would solve the labor question,

Doing away with saloons will certainly crab the diamond stud and ring industry, as about all other male species has gotten wise and quit wearing them,

President Wilson in his last note to the Americans said: Keep light wines and beers,

Many a politician now wishes he had had the nerve to have said the same thing,

Now are you going to follow Bryans advice or Pres Wilsons, I will string along with the one who has done something,

28

Simply take their two batting average,
Pres Wilson has been right a lot of times
But W J has yet to guess his first winner,

President says give us light wines and
beers, if they can get beer any lighter than
it is they will have to get a prop to hold it up,

Have to turn your glass upside down now
to keep it from flying away,

After drinking a bottle of this weak beer
you have to take a glass of water as a stimu-
lant,

That is what they fill these dirigible baloons with now,
its lighter than air,

You cant drink enough to get drunk on,
But you can drink enough to fly,

That peculiar taste that beer has nowadays
is the aniline dye they use to make it look
like beer,

The bartenders apology goes with every
bottle,

The only thing heavy about wine is the price,

There is a reward offered for a waiter that can make a cork pop like it used to,

Michigan has the natural ingredients of one of the best jags in the world, Take a bottle of any near beer and pour it over a bowl of grape nuts (michigans second commodity) [21] eat this hurriedly then take a five mile ride over one of their roads in a Ford and you have as good results as any souse would want,

They talk of shipping it in dry territory in coffins, Why my state of Okla, did that years ago, the way they got on to them was, There had been more bodies shipped to this town than the combined population of the whole state, One man got rich breaking up the coffins and selling the lumber as a by-product,

Now the bootleggers use aeroplanes to bring it in, The town marshal of my home Claremore Okla is rated as the leading Ace, he has brought down over 3000 quarts,[22]

30

You dont have to go any farther than our best ancient writers to prove that prohibition was unnecessary, look at old OMAR KHAY-HAM "The Pickled Philosopher of Persia" do you think Billy Sundays SLANG will live as long as Omars Philosophy has,[23]

In that verse something about "a loaf of bread a jug of Wine and Thou," Look how they have jagged those three things up on him, Bread,——they voted wheat so high nobody can eat bread, Wine will soon be gone and the wine they have got, if it had ever been handed to Omar I would hate to have read his book, Thou——I guess he meant a woman, Well she has the vote and she aint the same thou any more,[24]

He says he divorced old Barren reason and took the daughter of the Vine to spouse, Have you ever heard a dry say anything that smart,

I am against Divorces but there was a good legitimate reason and the first divorce case in history,[25]

Not only Omar but all the great men of the past had something on their hip all the

31

time, Caesar carried a canteen of Chianti that would make an Italian Restaurant proprietor envious, Shakespear, history says, when writing always had two bottles in front of him, now you know there was only one of them had Ink in it. He is the originator of the line "Bring on another Flagon of Ale,"

History says Nero fiddled while Rome burned, Now any man has got to drink to fiddle, and whoever listens to him fiddle has to drink more,

I have visited Washingtons old home at Mount Vernon, There are glasses in a case there that were never meant to drink water out of, Have a grape orchard there and I know they dident eat that many raisins, a basement down stairs and there were no furnaces in those days, What was in it?

The New York Times gave a prize for the best editorial on the war guess you would think some Teetotalar got it. WELL if Marse Henry Waterson is a total abstainer Mcadoo is a good railroad man,[26]

The Romans were the first people to discover after Noah any other reason for water,

32

*they put it in those beautiful Roman Baths
then built marble slabs to 'lay on and watch
it, You never saw a picture of a Roman in
the water in your life,*

Look at the mince pie, goodbye to it, We
dident kick what all they put in it (and they
put everything but mince) but when the old
brandy is shy why so long pie,

Speaking of prohibition we played in Bal-
timore which was wet the week the armistice
was signed, Washington was dry, Well Bal-
timore had such a big celebration and run
so short of stuff that they had to send over
to Washington for some more,

I had a friend who wanted a drink awful
bad when we were in Washington but he
couldent borrow a uniform from anybody,

The janitor who cleans up the Senators
and Congressmens rooms at the Capitol pays
a big price just for the empty bottle priv-
ilege,

**The foreign Embassys are supposed to be
the only wet spots, If I was a drinking man**

I would stop at the Oklahoma Embassy while there,

Big interests used to maintain a lobby with plenty of money there, Now they maintain a bar and get the same results,

Now you often hear a Wall Street man say "It cost me 6 quarts and over 100 cocktails to get that bill through,"

Now Congress says the women can vote, They use to could drink and not vote now they can vote and not drink,[27]

It will take them just as long to make up their minds who to vote for as it did to tell what to order to drink,

Most of them will vote for some guy named Martini just through force of habit,

If those women think they are going to get as much of a thrill around a voting booth; as they did around the old Punch Bowl they are going to be fooled,

Thats why the Anti Suffs fought it so hard
They knew that the old cocktail served in a
teacup at the afternoon tea, carried more real
authority than all the primaries ever held,

Prohibition takes all the joy out of voting,
Who wants to vote if theres no place to stop
on the way home, Besides one has to be
about half drunk to vote for most of the can-
didates they run nowadays,

**If some politicians wait for the sober vote
to elect them they are sunk,**

At first its going to feel kinder embarras-
sing to sell your vote while you are sober,

If they add the cost of the drinks a man
used to have to buy while dickering for your
vote to the price of the vote, It ought to
bring a fellow more real money now than
it did,

Votes will be higher as men wont be able
to sell them as often as they used to,

In the old days if you could keep the politician who was buying, drinking with you,

You could sometimes sell several times to him alone,

And its going to make an awful difference in counting them, More men have lost office through bad counting than through bad political policies,

A man with nothing on his hip but a patch aint liable to mistake one hundred for one thousand,

And if he is sober he aint near as liable to be asked to make said mistake,

A quart of old crow in the counting room at night has put more men in office than voters ever did,

If a man had to drink for every vote that has been torn up, or missplaced he wouldent have to worry about prohibition coming,

They lay all the divorces on to liquor, When its only bad judgement in picking em,

Some men have to drink to live with a woman some women have to drink to live with a man, most generally though they both have to drink to live with each other,

The drys as usual have it just wrong, It wont stop divorces it will stop marriages,

A couple sitting opposite at a table dont look near so good to each other over a water decanter as they do over two just emptied Champaign glasses,

Instead of weddings being jolly parties, From now on they are going to be as they should, very solemn affairs,

The old fashioned Justice or Minister that used to be woke up at three in the A M by a couple coming from some gay party wanting to get married, will have to look for some other occupation now,

If it will only cause better food and shorter speeches at banquets it will make up for all the bad it does,

And Poetry, they claim liquor is responsible for most all the poetry, and I believe it for it sounded like it,

See we have Russian Boomb throwing, if we have to take it to get that other Russian evil prohibition why I am in favor of giving them both back,[28]

These secret societies will be harder hit by it than anybody, As what they are taking away was their secret,

These reformers are always wanting to save you and if it wasent for them people wouldent need saving,

They cant lay Bolshevism on to booze, As at the late prices none of them could afford to buy it,

If you saw a man drunk in the old days it was a sign of no will power, But if you see one drunk now its a sure sign of wealth,

Somebody asked an old cattleman down home where I live if he was going to buy an Automobile (he was only worth a couple of hundred thousand) He said "No I aint, there are men in this county now who own automobiles that havent got a pint of whiskey in their house,"

Why not settle this Prohibition Fifty-Fifty, Let the Prohibitionists quit drinking,

Any time a dry is up talking just mention one word and he is through,—Russia,

If Pres Wilson wanted to get this League of Nations[29] through he should have taken some Prohibitionists with him they would have showed him how to get it through whether the people wanted it or not,

Some bird named Sheppard put this bill through congress, Leave it to a Texas Sheep herder to crab it,[30]

Turkey is the only other prohibition country in the world, If we enjoyed some of their
other privaleges it wouldent be so bad,[31]

**Somebody figured out now that we can
have 2 and three quarter percent beer, But
who wants to drink 37 and a half bottles to
be 100 percent drunk,**

Well I will jarr loose now, that is about
enough of this nonsense, I want to apologize
to the drys and say that maby I will write
another one on their side and have better
arguments, I dont drink and it dont make
any difference to me which side I am on,

I get paid for getting laughs and I found
out that the majority of the people would
laugh more if I kidded the drys,

BUT LOTS OF PEOPLE LAUGH ONE
WAY AND VOTE THE OTHER.

LOOK AT CONGRESS IT VOTED DRY AND DRINKS WET.

THE END

NOTES

[1]Rogers contracted with Harper and Brothers in 1919 to write six booklets, but only *The Cowboy Philosopher on the Peace Conference* (1919) and *The Cowboy Philosopher on Prohibition* (1919) were published. These volumes sold for sixty cents each.

[2]William Jennings Bryan (1860-1925). U.S. representative from Nebraska (1891-1895); secretary of state (1913-1915); unsuccessful Democratic presidential candidate in 1896, 1900, 1908. Leader of his party until 1912, when he helped nominate Woodrow Wilson. As secretary of state, Bryan, a total abstainer, promoted prohibition by never serving any alcoholic beverages at his diplomatic affairs.

[3]Albert Sidney Burleson (1863-1937). U.S. representative from Texas (1899-1913); postmaster general (1913-1921). He also served as chairman of the U.S. Telegraph and Telephone Administration thereby controlling the nation's wire service.

Rogers' humor about Burleson's unpopularity probably related to the severe restrictions which Burleson placed on the mailing privileges of magazines which he considered to be critical of the Wilson government's prosecution of the war.

[4]*The Four Horsemen of the Apocalypse* (1916) was a popular novel of the day written by Vincente Blasco Ibanez (1867-1928). The novel was adapted for the screen into a highly successful film starring Rudolph Valentino (1921). Both novel and film were popular because of their emphasis upon a contemporary theme of importance, the plight of young men during wartime. Ibanez also wrote *Blood and Sand* (1906) which was later made into a movie starring Rudolph Valentino (1922).

[5]Chautauqua was a traveling summer entertainment and cultural program held in large tents and usually lasting from three to five days. Programs were given in the afternoons and evenings, and numerous artists appeared. William Jennings Bryan was a popular Chautauqua speaker.

[6]Abbot Lawrence Lowell (1856-1943). Harvard professor of government (1900-1909); President of Harvard (1909-1933). Wrote several books on government; defender of academic freedom during the war.

[7]Rogers referred to audiences at the Ziegfeld Follies and the Midnight Frolic. In 1919 he performed downstairs at the Follies, and later each evening he performed again on the rooftop.

[8]Congress debated prohibition for more than a generation; by 1918 Congress had tired of being caught between the brewers and the Anti-Saloon League. Wartime prohibition had been in effect since July 1, 1919. In 1919, the Eighteenth Amendment outlining prohibition passed the Senate with a vote of 65 to 20, and the House by a vote of 282 to 128. The Amendment went into effect January 16, 1920, and lasted until the Twenty First Amendment repealed it in 1934.

⁹Jamaica Ginger was also known as "jake" and was one type of homemade liquor that paralyzed thousands of people. Bootleggers made fantastic profits even on inferior, lethal liquor such as "jake," "jackass brandy," and "soda pop moon."

¹⁰Thomas A. Edison (1847-1931). American inventor best known for the phonograph, and the improvement of the electric light bulb. During the twenties, Edison, Ford and other inventors were public idols. Thus they frequently served as subjects for Rogers' humor.

¹¹After World War I many areas of Europe were without adequate food supplies and the United States continued to help feed the war victims. Herbert Hoover established an impressive public record through his efforts to feed the starving continent. The humor of this line obviously involves a contrast between a real problem (starvation) and a manufactured problem (demon rum).

¹²Maine was first to have a law prohibiting the sale of liquor throughout the* state (1846 or 1851). Kansas passed a prohibition law in 1880, and tried to enforce prohibition from 1880 to 1949.

¹³Bevo was a non-alcoholic imitation beer which Anheuser-Busch produced in 1916.

¹⁴Douglas Haig (1861-1928). British field-marshal and commander of the British Expeditionary Force. In 1918 he directed the attack that broke the German defenses. Rogers here developed a pun relating a famous general of the last war with a famous Scotch, Haig and Haig.

¹⁵Cincinnati had a large German population strongly opposing prohibition and the closing of the city's beer gardens. Germans throughout the United States interpreted the prohibition movement as at least in part an anti-immigrant crusade.

¹⁶In June 1919, Columbus, Ohio hosted the Methodist Centenary Celebration. The Methodist Church was one of the staunchest supporters of prohibition.

¹⁷William Ashley "Billy" Sunday (1862-1935). Evangelist who reached the peak of his career between 1910-1920. He strongly supported the passage of the Eighteenth Amendment.

¹⁸The *George Washington* carried the American peace delegation to the Paris Peace Conference after World War I. Rogers referred to the fact that President Wilson chose only one Republican to the delegation, Henry White. Wilson's unwillingness to assemble a bi-partisan commission attracted much criticism.

¹⁹Secretary of State William Jennings Bryan, negotiated treaties with thirty nations to promote arbitration of disputes. He resigned his post in 1915, because he believed Wilson's protest to Germany for sinking the *Lusitania* was too strongly worded and that the protest would lead the United States into the war.

²⁰President Wilson believed that prohibition was a social and moral question not a political issue and that it should be settled by local option in each community.

²¹Battle Creek, Michigan, the location of the Kellogg

and General Food Companies, is known as the breakfast food capital of the world.

[22]Rogers actually was born in Oologah, Oklahoma, but his famous quip explained why he claimed Claremore as his home: "Only Indians could pronounce it." When registering at hotels, Rogers proudly listed his place of residence as "Claremore, Oklahoma." People then (and later) respected Rogers for his loyalty to his roots in Oklahoma.

[23]Omar Khayyam (1123) Persian poet and astronomer. Rogers referred here to the most famous stanza of *The Rubaiyat of Omar Khayyam*, a sybaritic poem of great popularity from 1890-1920. The *Rubaiyat* was published in countless illustrated gift editions.

[24]Many reformers had advocated equal suffrage since before the Civil War. During the early 1900's leadership temporarily fragmented, but the indispensable role of women in industry and society during World War I destroyed final resistance. President Wilson supported a suffrage amendment in 1917. The Nineteenth Amendment giving women the vote passed Congress in June, 1919, and became effective August, 1920. In this quip, Rogers referred to the many changes in post-war America: food was more expensive; "wine" in the sense of liquor was being pushed off the market; and the new woman was not the same passive creature of male fantasy which could be found in the *Rubaiyat*.

[25]Rogers often referred in amazement to the divorces and proudly announced that he was "the only motion picture star who has the same wife he originally started with." Note how literary the supposed unread "Cowboy Philosopher" is in this humorous play on words.

[26]Henry Watterson (1840-1921). American journalist; editor of *Louisville* (Ky.) *Courier-Journal* (1868-1918); won the Pulitzer prize (1917) for his editorial on U.S. declaration of war against the Central Powers. Strongly opposed women's suffrage, prohibition, and the League of Nations.

William G. McAdoo (1863-1941) U.S. secretary of the treasury (1913-1918); unsuccessfully sought Democratic nomination for president (1920, 1924); U.S. senator from California (1933-1939). The humor of this remark lies in McAdoo's role as director-general of the U.S. railroads during wartime, a post which inevitably brought him into conflict with individual lines.

[27]Those individuals opposing women's suffrage believed that politics were degrading, and therefore women should be denied the vote. Moreover, as women were not allowed to bear arms to defend the country they should not have a voice in national matters.

[28]After World War I, American coal and steel miners went on strike. Then a series of bombings prompted many Americans to believe that communists were responsible for labor unrest. The attorney general, A. Mitchell Palmer, conducted a swift and brutal witch hunt. Like Prohibition, this crusade against subversion was a negative, illiberal chapter in our national history. The causes of labor unrest had been poor wages and working conditions, not communist propaganda.

45

Russia and Canada forbade liquor during the war. Britain, France, and Germany severely regulated the use of liquor. The Moslem and Buddhist world also were officially under religious prohibition. More than half of the world's population lived under some form of prohibition.

[29]On January 9, 1918, President Woodrow Wilson presented his Fourteen Points to Congress. The last point provided for a "general association of nations" to guarantee political independence and territorial integrity. Wilson fought and compromised at the Versailles Peace Conference for the creation of the League of Nations only to see the U.S. Senate refuse to ratify it.

[30]Morris Sheppard (1875-1941). U.S. representative (1902-1913); U.S. senator (1913-1941). Ardent prohibitionist who led the Senate in support of the Eighteenth Amendment. As early as December, 1913, Sheppard had introduced a resolution supporting a constitutional amendment for Prohibition; in 1917 the Senate passed the Sheppard Bill prohibiting the manufacture, importation, or sale of liquor in the District of Columbia.

[31]Rogers referred to the Turkish custom of maintaining a harem. Polgamy in Turkey became unlawful after 1928.

THE EVOLVING CAREER OF WILL ROGERS

The Cowboy Philosopher on Prohibition and its companion volume *The Cowboy Philosopher on the Peace Conference* were published at a time when Will Rogers' horizons were broadening. He was working in Ziegfeld's *Midnight Frolic* the night World War One was declared. Three days later (April 5, 1917), he made a troubled President Wilson smile at a Washington, D.C. theatre.

In August, 1918, at Fort Lee, New Jersey, Rogers completed his first film—a screen adaptation of Rex Beach's western story, *Laughing Bill Hyde*. Rogers then signed with Goldwyn Pictures in Culver City, California at $2,250 per week, beginning in June, 1919. In May, just prior to departing with his family (to include two horses) by train for the West Coast, the cowboy philosopher contracted with Harper and Brothers to write six booklets. By June, 1920, Rogers had appeared in at least seven films and had sent in his first syndicated commentaries on a presidential convention. Thus, Rogers had made speedy changes from vaudeville-cowboy to a national film and journalism talent.

After several years with various Wild West shows, Will Rogers adapted his cowboy act to the stage. His earliest routine was strictly a display of trick roping. With Buck McKee and a horse named Teddy as living "props," he made a successful tour of vaudeville theaters of the United States and Europe (1905-1915). Anyone who has had an opportunity to see Rogers' silent film, *The Roping Fool* (1919), can testify to his use of complex loops and multiple ropes. Many experts on the subject believe that this level of proficiency with the lasso will never again be attained.

Rogers was invited to join Florenz Ziegfeld's

Will Rogers with Buck McKee and horse named Teddy during vaudeville tours (1905-1915).

Midnight Frolic in 1915. The *Frolic* was an evening version of the *Follies,* but specifically designed for an exclusive late night audience.

To any observer of his career and personality, Rogers' exact place in the world of Ziegfeld remains a paradox. His Oklahoma accent, rural metaphors, and crackerbarrel insights were colored with rustic simplicity and directness. Yet the *Frolic* environment glittered with some of the most exotic creations of male fantasy:

Girls ran about dressed as switchboards, and telephones on each table connected each customer to the switchboard of his choice. Some girls dressed as

Zeppelins, with sweeping searchlights moving over them against an urban background of a burning city . . . . A balcony was suspended from the ceiling by chains. The balcony floor was of plate glass on which the girls danced. The stage was moveable, thrusting out between the diners by means of special machinery.

Busby Berkeley is today known for his spectacular displays of women in film, but Berkeley was only carrying over into a mass medium ideas which he had invented as a Ziegfeld associate for the *Follies*.

In the midst of all this glitter, Will Rogers reminded the industrialists, bankers, and foreign and domestic visitors in the audience of a simpler past and a different scale of values which America of the 1920's, in its orgy of materialism, was trying to sweep under the national rug. The newspapers billed Rogers variously. At this point in his career, the rope had become less of a tool than a metaphor.

Rogers "out of uniform"—but distinctly in good company—with W. C. Fields, Eddie Cantor and Harry Kelley.

49

The verbal portion of one New York journal *Follies* advertisement emphasized Rogers' "genius" and his abilities as "America's own Humorist." The cartoon emphasized the jovial grin, symbolic of his wit; the rope framed his face for a touch of western flavor.

The *Follies* routine consisted of a great variety of sketches, tableaus, and musical numbers, and like other performers, Rogers was asked to do more than twirl a rope and comment on the news. He was most distinctly "out of uniform"—but still in good company—with W. C. Fields, Eddie Cantor and Harry Kelley. In examining the visual documents that remain from his *Follies* career, it is difficult to determine whether Rogers was popular because he was part of the fantasy world of Ziegfeld, or because he served as an earthy counterpoint to the urbane comedy and lavish display Ziegfeld constructed. Rogers was not visually distinguished from the other entertainers represented in "Flipping the Follies in Free Fantasia." That he could lend his efforts to a display of beautiful females was obvious. Very few cowboys have been lucky enough to share an evening with such attractive co-workers.

Yet much of Rogers' humor was based upon his ability to pose as an innocent outsider to the values of sophisticated America which would have responded favorably to the entertainment Ziegfeld and his associates assembled. Two cartoons effectively established this contrast between Rogers and the Ziegfeld setting. In the first, Rogers, on stage as the shy but insightful visitor from the untainted American heartland, ridiculed Ziegfeld's elaborate showmanship with the line about the "poultry" moving behind him, thus verbally associating rural life with the high society theater sport (female display). In the second, Rogers quipped about the inordinate interest shown by wealthy male patrons of the *Follies*. While the women appeared in active

50

Rogers was not visually distinguished from the other entertainers represented in "Flipping the Follies in Free Fantasia."

(almost frenetic) attitude and other entertainers were pictured in the midst of various contrived acts, Rogers was shown in a reflective mood. It almost appeared that at any moment his rope would drop

Rogers associating rural life with the high society theater sport (female display).

51

Rogers was shown in a reflective mood.

to the floor, and the scratching stop. In a spontaneous gulp, some celebrity in the audience or some absurdity from the daily news would be invoked, thereby sending the audience into hysterics.

The visual contrast between Rogers the cowboy and the "Fine Feathers Girl" comments on where Americans in the Twenties hoped they were going; Will Rogers reminded them where they had been.